Diana: I'm Going to be Me

The People's Princess Revealed in Her Own Words

Diana: I'm Going to be Me

The People's Princess Revealed in Her Own Words

Published by
Barzipan Publishing
www.barzipan.com

©Phil Dampier 2017

ISBN 978-0-992613-39-6

Printed and bound by Interak Printing House, Poland

CIP Data: A catalogue record for this book is available from the
British Library.

Diana: I'm Going to be Me

The People's Princess Revealed in Her Own Words

Phil Dampier

Barzipan Publishing
*not what you'd expect

Phil Dampier has been writing about the Royal Family for 30 years.

Between 1986 and 1991 he covered the royal beat for *The Sun*, Britain's biggest-selling daily newspaper, and frequently engaged in conversations with Princess Diana while reporting her weekly duties, as well as numerous holidays.

As a freelance journalist for the last 25 years, he has travelled to more than 60 countries, following members of the House of Windsor, and his articles have been published in dozens of newspapers and magazines worldwide.

He often appears on radio and TV, and gave expert analysis for Global National TV of Canada during their coverage of the Duke and Duchess of Cambridge's tour of British Columbia in 2016.

CONTENTS

By the same author: (with Ashley Walton)

Prince Philip: Wise Words and Golden Gaffes, Barzipan Publishing 2012

White House Wit, Wisdom and Wisecracks, Barzipan Publishing 2013

SOURCES AND ACKNOWLEDGEMENTS

I personally witnessed some of Diana's comments. Others have come from newspaper and magazine reports, and I am also grateful for material from the following books:

Diana, Sarah Bradford (Penguin 2006)

Diana: Closely Guarded Secret, Ken Wharfe with Robert Jobson (Michael O'Mara 2002)

Diana Her True Story, Andrew Morton (Michael O'Mara 1992)

Diana Her True Story – In Her Own Words, Andrew Morton (Michael O'Mara 1997)

Diana in Private – The Princess Nobody Knows, Lady Colin Campbell (Smith Gryphon 1992)

Diana in Search of Herself, Sally Bedell Smith (Random House 1999)

Diana, The Last Word, Simone Simmons with Ingrid Seward (Orion 2005)

I'll Tell The Jokes Arthur, Arthur Edwards (Blake Publishing 1993)

Once Upon A Time, Mary Clarke (Sidgwick and Jackson 1994)

Portraits of a Princess: Travels with Diana, Patrick Jephson and Kent Gavin (Sidgwick & Jackson 2004)

Royal Service, Stephen Barry (Avon Books 1983)

The Definitive Diana, Sally Moore (Coronet Books 1992)

The Diana Chronicles, Tina Brown (Century 2007)

The Truth, Judy Wade (Blake Publishing 2001)

FOREWORD

It is extraordinary to think that 20 years have now passed since the death of Princess Diana, a tragedy which brought forth a tsunami of grief around the world.

There are young married couples pushing babies in prams who were not even born when Diana was killed in a Paris car crash on 31 August 1997.

But for many of us who remember where we were when we heard the news of her shocking demise, the days that followed live fresh in the memory.

In this book, the first comprehensive collection of her quotes, I have tried to show this complex and vulnerable figure in the round, with all her strengths and weaknesses.

Scarred by her parents' divorce when she was young, Diana was deeply insecure and far from perfect.

She came close to inflicting permanent damage on the Royal Family, was branded a marriage wrecker after a series of affairs, and often fell out with those closest to her.

But she was also a fashion icon, a trailblazer in campaigns fighting AIDS and land mines, and ,most importantly, was a loving mother who left two sons whom she would now be immensely proud of.

Pitched into royal life aged just 20 when she married Prince Charles, Diana was already full of hope and full of doubts – and her own words often contradict themselves.

Despite her faults – or perhaps because of them – she was admired and adored by millions in every continent, and the outpouring of affection after her death was one of the most remarkable events in the second half of the 20th century.

So sit back and celebrate the amazing life of this never-to-be forgotten woman – the beautiful, beguiling, flawed but uniquely enchanting Diana.

Most of these quotes are in chronological order, but some, for example about childhood, were spoken some time after the events they describe.

Phil Dampier

May 2017

BEFORE CHARLES
1961–1981

BEFORE CHARLES
1961-1981

'My first memory is really the smell of the inside of my pram. It was plastic and the hood smelled of it.'

'Vivid memory. I was born at home not in hospital.'

As a child: 'When I grow up I'm going to marry Prince Andrew – he's my friend.'

On schooldays: 'We used to be very naughty and slide down the back of the bath.'

Good at netball, she said later: 'It was much easier for me to get the ball in the net as I was so tall.'

'I wasn't a good child in the sense that I had horns in my ears. I was always looking for trouble.'

'The biggest disruption was when Mummy decided to leg it.'

When Diana was sent to boarding school aged nine she told her father: *'If you leave me now, you don't love me.'*

'I remember seeing my father slap my mother across the face. I was hiding behind the door. Mum cried a lot.'

'The divorce helped me to relate to anyone else who is upset in their family life, whether it be stepfather syndrome or mother or whatever, I understand it.'

At the age of 16, Diana met Prince Charles at the Spencer family home while her sister Sarah was going out with him.

Told to school friends at West Heath in Sevenoaks, Kent: *'I've met him! At last I've met him.'*

Her verdict: *'Pretty amazing.'*

Told to her childhood nanny Mary Clarke: *'My only ambition is to fall in love, get married and have lots of children.'*

'I would never marry unless I was really really in love.'

'I never want to be divorced.'

Told to Mary Clarke 18 months before her marriage to Charles: *'The love of my life is to dance and sing. But I have an awful voice and I'm like an elephant when I dance, so no one watches me.'*

On her early ambition to be a ballet dancer: *'I overshot the height by a long way. I couldn't imagine some man trying to lift me up above his arms.'*

As a teenager she dated several boys but none became lovers and she said: *'I knew I had to keep myself tidy for what lay ahead.'*

In September 1978 Diana was staying with friends when she told them she had a premonition her father would soon *'drop down.'*

'If he dies, he will die immediately, otherwise he will survive,' she said.

The next day, Earl Spencer collapsed with a massive brain haemorrhage from which he did recover, and three years later he walked her up the aisle.

Invited to a shooting weekend at Sandringham in February 1978, she told a friend who said she might become Queen: *'I doubt it. Can you imagine me swanning around in kid gloves and a ballgown?'*

In July 1980 Diana met Charles at a house party in Petworth, West Sussex. Sitting on a hay bale after a polo match she referred to the murder of Earl Mountbatten the previous year. She said: *'You looked so sad when you walked up the aisle at the funeral. It was the most tragic thing I've ever seen. My heart bled for you when I watched it. I thought: It's wrong, you are lonely, you should be with somebody to look after you.'*

'I'll read almost anything I can get my hands on from women's magazines to Charles Dickens.'

On the famous photo taken at the nursery where she worked when her legs showed through her skirt because of the light: *'I ended up in the papers looking like I had Steinway piano legs.'*

On her first visit to Balmoral to meet the Queen: *'I was shitting bricks. I was terrified. I had never stayed at Balmoral before and I wanted to get it right.'*

As speculation grew about their relationship, Diana told a reporter on November 28, 1980: *'I'd like to marry soon. What woman doesn't want to marry eventually?*

'Next year? Why not? I don't think nineteen is too young. It depends on the person.'

Asked if Charles had proposed, she blushed and replied: *'I can't say yes or no to that. I can't confirm or deny it.'*

When Charles proposed to her: *'He said, "Will you marry me?' and I laughed and I remember thinking, "This is a joke".'*

'And I said, "Yeah, okay," and laughed and he was deadly serious.'

'He said, "You do realise that one day you will be Queen," and a voice said to me inside, "You won't be Queen but you'll have a tough role."'

'I said, "Yes," and he said, "I love you so much – whatever love means."'

'He said it then so I thought that was great, I thought he meant that. And he ran upstairs and rang his mother.'

When Diana told her mother that she was going to marry Charles and that she loved him, Mrs Frances Shand Kydd asked: *'Love him, or what he is?'*

Diana replied: *'What's the difference?'*

Charles and Diana were engaged on 24 February 1981 and interviewed in the garden of Buckingham Palace. Asked if they were in love Diana said: *'Of course,'* **before Charles famously added:** *'Whatever love means.'*

Four days later Diana wrote to a well-wisher: *'Reading through all the letters, it's amazing how many people have said that married life is the best – I wonder if I'll be saying that in twenty years' time!'*

On her sapphire and diamond engagement ring: *'I can't get used to wearing it yet. The other day I even scratched my nose with it because it's so big – the ring, I mean.'*

'With Prince Charles beside me, I can't go wrong.'

'It's always nice when there are two of you and there's someone there to help you.'

'The Prince has made everything far easier for me.'

Note to her former flatmates after she got engaged: *'For God's sake ring me up – I'm going to need you.'*

Why Charles didn't go to Wimbledon to watch tennis with her: *'It's because he can never sit still. He is like a great big baby – but one day I hope to calm him down enough to enjoy it.'*

Just before the wedding she was sitting in a car when she saw a huge poster of herself. Breaking down in tears she told an aide: *'I can't take this anymore.'*

To a blind woman at a Buckingham Palace garden party just before the wedding: *'Do you want to feel my engagement ring? I'd better not lose it before Wednesday or they won't know who I am.'*

After choosing her engagement ring at Windsor Castle when she dined with the Queen she told Charles's valet Stephen Barry: *'There was a whole tray of rings waiting for me from Garrards* [the royal jewellers]. *The Queen's eyes popped when I picked out the largest one.'*

'It's a beautiful sapphire with diamonds – I love it.'

On the wedding rehearsal: *'Everybody was fighting. I got my heel stuck in some grating and everyone was saying "Hurry up Diana," and I said, "I can't, I'm stuck!"'*

The day before the wedding she joked: *'I'm going to videotape it. Then I'll be able to run back over the best bits – and when it comes to the part that says, "I will" I'm going to take that out and put something else!'*

'They put me in a bedroom overlooking the Mall, which meant I didn't get any sleep.'

On the enormous breakfast she ate on her wedding day: *'I hope that stops my tummy rumbling in St Paul's.'*

The couple married on 29 July 1981 and Diana sat next to her father for the carriage ride.

'Father was so thrilled that he waved himself stupid,' she said later.

'It was wonderful.'

Told to James Hewitt at his mother's house in Devon. *'As I was walking down the aisle of St Paul's on my father's arm I thought, "What on earth am I doing here?"'*

She later told a friend: *'It was heaven, amazing, wonderful, though I was so nervous when I was walking up the aisle that I swore my knees would knock and make a noise.'*

As she walked up the aisle she spotted Camilla Parker Bowles, whom she had already realised was a love threat, in the congregation.

'I was furious,' she later recalled.

'I wanted to turn and run.'

'If I'd had the courage I would have hitched up my dress and bolted out of the church.'

As Diana arrived at the altar, Charles said: *'You look beautiful,'* and she replied, *'Beautiful for you.'*

Making her wedding vows, Diana nervously got Charles's names mixed up, and vowed to take *'Philip Charles Arthur George'* as her husband.

'I was so in love with my husband that I couldn't take my eyes off him.'

'I just absolutely thought I was the luckiest girl in the world.'

'I had to see the funny side, otherwise I would have burst into tears.'

'I felt like a sacrificial lamb.'

Letter to her former nanny Mary Clarke just before her wedding: *'To be engaged for six months is quite something and definitely to be avoided.'*

MARRIAGE:
1981–1992

MARRIAGE: 1981–1992

On her honeymoon aboard the Royal Yacht *Britannia* in the Mediterranean: *'I wanted to sing and dance and do exciting things, but all he wanted to do was take it easy, read and sunbathe.'*

'I was bored, it was like being stuck with an eighty-year-old man.'

The honeymoon continued at Balmoral with Diana later writing to a friend: *'It's heavenly up here, just having the opportunity to do what you like and walk for miles.'*

'I've vanished down many a hole – the husband having not realised, typical!'

'One moment I was a nobody, the next minute I was Princess of Wales, mother, media toy, member of this family and it was just too much for one person to handle.' Said to friends looking back on becoming a royal.

Not long into her marriage she wrote to former nanny Mary Clarke: *'I adore being married and having someone to devote my time to.'*

When Mary's husband moved to Uganda, Diana wrote: *'How hopeless I would feel if my other half went away.'*

Just six months after her wedding, Diana told Mary Clarke: *'I might even have to learn to ride a horse, Mary, as it is the only time I will see my husband on his own.'*

On an early visit to Balmoral she wrote to a friend: *'I feel totally out of place here.'*

'I sometimes wonder what on earth I have got myself into. I feel so small, lonely, so out of my depth.'

She told a friend: *'Christ, you have no idea how much the country bores me.'*

'Balmoral is as deadly as a graveyard.'

According to Lady Colin Campbell in her book *Diana in Private*, rows soon began with Charles.

On one occasion he was seen driving off in a Range Rover at Balmoral with Diana running alongside shouting: *'Yes, dump me like garbage. Leave me on my own again. Run off and have lunch with your precious mummy.'*

During another spat she was heard to scream: *'What am I supposed to do all day while you're off enjoying yourself?' Die of boredom? You call yourself a husband, some husband you are!'*

To Charles's valet Stephen Barry: *'Don't you think he's a bit formal, the way he dresses? Perhaps we'll try and change things.'*

On what she expected royal life to be: *'Thirty percent fantastic, seventy percent sheer slog.'*

On public engagements: *'Imagine having to go to a wedding every day of your life – as the bride. Well, that's a bit what it's like.'*

'No one helped me learn the ropes… I was just pushed into the fire.'

On switching on the Christmas Lights in London: *'I had to make a speech in front of the whole of Regent Street. I was shit scared.'*

'It was horrendous at first. I didn't know whether to go out of the door first.'

'I didn't know whether your handbag should be in your left hand or your right. I was terrified really.'

When pregnant with William she suffered terribly from morning sickness and told a friend: *'Nobody told me I would feel like this.'*

'I don't eat breakfast.'

Suffering from acute morning sickness and tormented by Charles's relationship with Camilla Parker Bowles, Diana later admitted: *'I threw myself down the stairs at Sandringham.'*

'The Queen comes out, absolutely horrified, shaking – she was just so frightened.'

'I knew I wasn't going to lose the baby but I was quite bruised around the stomach.'

'Charles went riding and when he came back, you know, it was just dismissal, total dismissal.'

'I wanted to talk to Charles about something, he wouldn't listen to me, said I was crying wolf. So I picked up his penknife off his dressing table and scratched myself heavily down my chest and both thighs.'

'There was a lot of blood and he hadn't made any reaction whatsoever.'

'I ate kippers all the time when I was pregnant with William.'

Three months after William's birth in 1982 she wrote to a friend: *'William has brought us such happiness and contentment and consequently I can't wait for masses more.'*

On Charles as a father: *'He's a doting daddy and does everything perfectly.'*

Arriving for a tour of Australia in 1983, Prince William was immediately taken away by a nanny to a sheep station. When a wag in the crowd shouted: *'Aaw, Billy the Kid's feet haven't touched Australian soil,'* Diana laughed and replied, *'Goodness, he isn't the Pope you know!'*

On the same tour, a mum in the crowd told her she envied her because she had a nanny to look after William. *'Oh no, I envy you,'* said Diana. *'You can be with your baby all the time.'*

Talking to a one-armed man in the crowd in Australia: *'I bet you have fun chasing the soap around the bath!'*

'When we came back from the six week tour of Australia and New Zealand I was a different person.'

'I was more gown up, more mature, but not anything like the process I was going to go through in the next four or five years.'

Said to friends: 'I'd love to be able to run along a beach without a policeman following me.'

'The trouble with being a Princess is that it is so hard to have a pee.'

'Being a Princess is not all it's cracked up to be.'

On the Queen: 'I have the best mother-in-law in the world.'

'I was accused very early on of stopping him [**Charles**] shooting and hunting – that was total rubbish. He suddenly went all vegetarian and wouldn't kill – his family thought he had gone mad.'

'I've always admired Margo [**Princess Margaret**] as I call her. I love her to bits and she's been wonderful to me from day one.'

On Princess Anne: 'I'm her biggest fan because what she crams into a day I could never achieve.'

'We've always hit it off very well and I think she's just
marvellous… she works ten times harder than me and
deserves every bit of credit coming her way.'

**Laughing about not being able to behave the way she
once did:** 'I think that's probably just as well – if you knew
how I used to behave!'

While pregnant with Prince Harry: 'I haven't felt well
since day one. I don't think I'm made for the production
line… but it's all worth it in the end.'

'Harry appeared by a miracle.'

'We were very very close to each other the six weeks before
Harry was born, the closest we've ever, ever been and ever
will be.'

'Then, suddenly, as Harry was born it just went bang, our
marriage, the whole thing went down the drain.'

'Charles always wanted a girl.'

'First comment was, "Oh God, it's a boy," second comment,
"and he's even got red hair".'

'Something inside me closed off. By then I knew he had
gone back to his lady but somehow we'd managed to have
Harry.'

Shortly after Harry's birth in September 1984, Diana wrote to a friend: *'William has totally taken over his brother and Charles and I are hardly allowed near as he covers Harry in an endless supply of hugs and kisses.'*

'My husband knows so much about rearing children that I've suggested he has the next one and I'll sit back and give advice.'

'I breast fed William for three weeks and Harry for eleven weeks.'

'If men had to have babies, they would only have one each.'

On looking after her young sons: *'It's all hard work and no pay.'*

'By Sunday I am a stretcher case.'

'They are little minxes.'

Asked on a walkabout when she would have a third child: *'I'm not a production line you know.'* **(1985)**

'Hugs can do a great amount of good – especially for children.'

Defending the cost of her outfits for tours: *'I couldn't go round in a leopard skin.'*

'We're open-minded about William and his education because the bad luck about being number one is trial and error. Number two skates in quite nicely.

'So we're still learning all the tricks of the trade.'

On the day of Prince William's confirmation: 'It's a very important day in his life. One day he will be the head of the Church of England and and I want him to understand fully all the responsibilities he will have.'

'It's important for everyone to have something to believe in.'

On her children: 'They will not be hidden upstairs with the nanny.'

'A mother's arms are so much more comforting than anyone else's.'

'I want my children to have as normal a life as possible.'

'It's so important to me that they grow up not only knowing who they are, but what the world's really like.

'I want them to realise not everybody has a Range Rover and a country house.'

At the 1985 Live Aid concert, David Bowie asked Diana to join stars on stage for the finale. 'I might be able to sing a bit of God Save the Queen, but that's as far as my vocal talents go,' **she said.**

At fittings with couturier Jasper Conran, just three years into her marriage, Diana broke down in tears pleading: *'Please make me look sexy for my husband.'*

'I feel my role is supporting my husband whenever I can, and always being behind him, encouraging him.'

'And also, being a mother and a wife. And that's what I try to achieve.

'Whether I do is another thing, but I do try.'

'My husband has taught me everything I know.'

On Charles and his interests: *'He loves his garden, but as soon as he's finished sorting out every inch of it he will get bored with it and take up something else. He's like that.'*

'I am a perfectionist with myself, though not necessarily with everyone else.'

Letter to a friend: *'You must know only too well that what a female needs more than anything (apart from a husband) is a mass of hangers for the clothes.'*

Diana developed the eating disorder bulimia, and was often sick, much to the dismay of Charles.
'I don't know what my husband fed her [the Queen]. *He definitely told her about my bulimia and she told*

everybody that was the reason why our marriage had backed up ... because of Diana's eating and it must be so difficult for Charles.'

At the 1986 Expo World Fair in Vancouver, Canada, a weak Diana thought she was going to faint and told Charles: *'Darling, I think I'm about to disappear,'* **and slid down his side.**

After several members of staff left, Diana told royal reporter James Whitaker in 1985: *'I want you to understand that I am not responsible for any sackings. I just don't sack people.'*

Told to Captain James Hewitt in 1986: *'I'm terrified of horses. I fell off a pony and broke my arm when I was a child and I've been a bag of nerves ever since. I'm not sure I ever want to ride again.'*

'There is far too much about me in the newspapers, far too much. It horrifies me when there's more important things, like what goes on in the hospices, or there's been a bomb or something.'

'The Queen is always surrounded by corgis so you get the feeling you are standing on a moving carpet.'

When one of the Queen's corgis was licking her leg, Diana barked to a friend: *'Get it out of here, it's licking all my tan off!'*

'I simply treat the press as though they were children.'

'You know everything about me except how many fillings I've got – and I'm not telling you that.'

When William was to be a pageboy at Sarah Ferguson's wedding to Prince Andrew in 1986: *'I'm going to put down a line of Smarties in the aisle at Westminster Abbey so that William will know where to stand, and he's got to stay there... he's terribly excited.'*

'I only hope he behaves in the Abbey. He will rise to the occasion, at least, I hope he will!'

'You won't need me any more, now that you've got Fergie.'

'I got terribly jealous of Fergie and she got jealous of me.'

To Fergie, when she joined the Royal Family in 1986: *'Be delightful, but be discreet.'*

'Life at Buckingham Palace isn't too bad but too many formal dinners – yuk!'

On some palace courtiers: *'It was as if Charles was married to them, not me, and they are so patronising it drives me mad.'*

On Capital Radio: *'It's the best.'*

'I've gone off EastEnders and now I prefer Brookside.'

On TV chat show host Jonathan Ross: *'I've sat next to him twice at functions and I think he's wonderful.'*

On being wounded by press criticism: *'You think, oh gosh, I don't want to go out and do my engagement this morning.'*

'Nobody wants to see me, help, panic.'

'But you have got to push yourself out and remember that some people hopefully won't remember everything they read about you.'

On calling love rival Camilla Parker Bowles the 'Rottweiler': *'Because she looks like a dog, and once she has got her teeth into someone she won't let go.'*

She told her hairdresser Richard Dalton: *'Charles must be wearing beer goggles to have an affair with Camilla.'*

In May 1986 she told Japanese journalists: *'I don't know why there are all these stories saying I am too thin – I am eating a lot.'*

'I have an enormous appetite, despite what people say, and so has William. He takes after his mother.'

'I would walk miles for a bacon sandwich.'

Asked by *Dangerous Liaisons* star John Malkovitch after watching a post-sex breakfast scene in the movie: *'Is it like that for breakfast at the Palace?'* Diana replied: *'No, but it beats reading the papers!'*

She also told him: *'I'm not easily shocked!'*

To President Mario Soares at a banquet in Portugal 1987: *'If I get cold, will you warm me up?'*

After he offered her his dinner jacket in the chilly Palace, she said, twanging his braces: *'You're a socialist aren't you? You should be wearing red braces.'*

To a photographer at a 1987 cocktail party in Madrid: *'When we first got married we were everyone's idea of the world's most perfect couple. Now they say we're leading separate lives. The next thing I know I'll read in some newspaper that I've got a black Catholic lover.'*

Told to writer and historian Paul Johnson: *'What I wanted to be before I got married was an air hostess, but I wasn't educated or intelligent enough.'*

'I cannot diet – I am not strong-willed enough.' **(1988)**

Letter to beautician Janet Filderman: *'I wish that I could cope with the media and people's thirst for knowledge of us, but after six years I find everything that much more of a struggle and just cannot see a light at the end of the tunnel.'*

'I know there are a million people worse off than me and that I should do all I can for them but at the end of the day I have to live with myself and emotionally at the moment I am upside down and confused (so boring for those around me) and putting on this act is desperate but if it keeps people off my back then surely it must be worth it.'

In 1987: *'Just because I go out without my husband it doesn't mean that my marriage is on the rocks.'*

In July 1988, Diana fan Paul Ratcliffe, 17, asked her if he could kiss her cheek. *'You'd better kiss my hand – you never know where it might lead if you kiss me on the cheek,'* **she replied.**

'William is just like me – always in trouble.'

'William's got a good brain, especially considering how hopeless both his parents were. He's a deep thinker.'

'I don't keep secrets from my boys.'

'I just can't win. They either accuse me of spending too much on my clothes or of wearing the same outfit all the time.'

'My clothes are not my priority.'

'I enjoy bright colours and my husband likes me to look smart and presentable, but fashion isn't my big thing at all.'

'Clothes are for the job. They've got to be practical. Sometimes I can be a little outrageous, which is quite nice, but only sometimes.'

'Hats give me confidence.'

On high-heeled shoes by Jimmy Choo and Manolo Blank: 'I call them my tart's trotters.'

Said to friends at a party: 'I'd love to have my nose fixed – it's too big.'

To astounded journalists: 'Do you remember how I was? I used to have lots up top, remember? Well, it's all gone now I've had my boys, hasn't it?'

Told to a volunteer hairdresser at a hospice 1986: *'I would love to have my hair cut short but they won't let me because I need to wear it long... it goes better with tiaras and hats. The compromise is lots of lacquer.'*

In 1990 she did have a new, shorter style and said: *'I feel much cooler.'*

'What have the newspapers ever done for me?'

'Brain the size of a pea I've got.'

After hitting her head on a low doorway: *'No sense, no feeling – thick as two short planks, me.'*

On her head: *'It may be large, but there's not much in it.'*

On George Michael: *'He's gay – what a waste!'*

On supermodel Naomi Campbell: *'That girl is truly beautiful.'*

'She is so exotic and glamorous that an old black bin-liner would look good on her.'

On a walkabout when wearing a fake-fur wrap over her hands to keep warm, she told a woman in the crowd: *'I've got a mouse in my muff!'*

'I want to bring them [William and Harry] *up with security, not to anticipate things, because they will be disappointed.'*

'That's made my own life so much easier.'

'I hug my children to death and get into bed with them at night. I always feed them love and affection – it's so important.'

On a trip to Italy a photographer asked her why she had worn an old gown to the opera. *'Oh, I suppose you'd like it better if I came naked?'* she replied.

Talking about William and Harry to Inspector Ken Wharfe when he first became her Scotland Yard protection officer: *'I know it is going to be tough Ken, given who they are, but it is so so important to me that they grow up not only knowing who they are, but what the world is really like.'*

'So, Ken – basically you are my last line of defence?'

'So, does that mean you will take a bullet for me?'

Said to Charles during rows, according to Ken Wharfe: *'If only I was as important as your garden. Go on, talk to your flowers!'*

Told to Ken Wharfe: *'After Harry was born our marriage just died. What could I do? I tried but he just did not want me. He just wanted her, always her, do you know I don't think I ever stood a chance.'*

On holiday in Majorca, Charles and Diana stayed with King Juan Carlos of Spain.

'I think the King fancies me,' Diana told Ken Wharfe. *'It's awful. He's frightfully charming but, you know, a little too attentive.'*

'He is very tactile. I told my husband and he says I am just being silly.'

Also to Ken Wharfe: *'I used to blame myself, to hate myself. Nobody in the Royal Family ever praised me, can you believe that? After all I've done for that family.'*

Told to Ken Wharfe in Majorca, 1988: *'Do you know we have not slept in the same bed for years, Ken?'*

While walking along the River Dee at Balmoral with Ken Wharfe: *'It makes me sick. Everybody says I loathe this place but I love Scotland. It's just the pervading atmosphere generated by those Germans* [the royals] *that drains me.'*

'I do so like men in uniform.'

'When I'm nervous I tend to giggle.'

'I'm a normal person, hopefully, who loves life.'

'I've got ears like a bat.'

'I like playing bridge but I'm no good – I talk too much.'

Said to Cliff Richard: *'It's so nice to get home and have a bowl of custard.'*

At a banquet in Indonesia: *'I don't like champagne.'*

At the 40th birthday party of Camilla Parker Bowles's sister Annabel Elliott, Diana confronted Camilla, whom she suspected of having an affair with Prince Charles, and told her: *'I'm sorry I'm in the way and it must be hell for both of you, but I do know what is going on.*

'Don't treat me like an idiot.'

In a prophetic speech as President of Barnardo's the children's charity, in 1988: *'I know that family life is extremely important, and, as a mother of two small boys, I think we may have to find a securer way of helping our* *children – to nurture and prepare them to face life as stable and confident adults.'*

'The pressures and demands on all of us are enormous.'

'Today few children lose parents through early death, but many do experience that loss through divorce, and increasingly more complicated families result from separation and remarriage.'

In 1989 she told a Barnardo's conference: *'I know many parents with handicapped children have a tremendous worry as to what will happen to your child when you are no longer here to cope. Who will bother about their likes and dislikes, remember special occasions like their birthdays?'*

'As a mother of two small and rather inquisitive boys, I know how easy it is for accidents to happen!'

'It's amazing how much happiness a small child brings to people.'

In March 1991 she said: *'Contrary to what you may have heard I'd like lots and lots more children.'*

A few days later she was touring a children's hospital and was asked if she would like a daughter.

'*Yes I would love one,*' she replied, adding: '*I wonder if the world is ready for another me.*'

On working with the terminally ill and doing bereavement counselling: '*I love it, I can't wait to get into it. It's like a hunger.*'

'*Helping people in need is a good and essential part of my life.*'

'*I am all about caring, I have always been like that.*'

'*I want to walk into a room, be it a hospital for the dying or a hospital for sick children, and feel that I am needed. I want to do, not just be.*'

Said to friends in 1990: '*Life is just a journey.*'

On acupuncture, which she was undergoing once a week in 1990: '*It helps me to stay calm and not panic.*'

At a reception on board the Royal Yacht *Britannia* in 1990, Diana told Daulla Bello, wife of Nigeria's Chief Justice, who had eight children of her own: '*I'd like three more babies – but I haven't told my husband yet.*'

'*I grew up in a family of four, but I would like one extra – I think five children make the perfect family.*'

To a 14 year-old Welsh schoolboy flooded out of his home in 1990: *'I bet you are glad there's no school and you don't have to have baths!'*
Letter to her lover Captain James Hewitt when he was in the desert during the Gulf War 1991: *'Bet you'll never go on a beach holiday again!'*

As her marriage crumbled, Diana gave broad hints that all was not well. On her 30th birthday in July 1991 she was at a fundraising lunch at the Savoy Hotel and said: *'I'm going to celebrate my birthday at home alone with the only man in my life tonight – Prince Harry.'*

To UK's ambassador to France Sir Ewen Fergusson in Paris 1992: *'We're* [she and her sister Sarah] *both worried about getting varicose veins because mummy's got them.'*

Told to a photographer in Cairo, Egypt. 1992: *'I hate polo. I don't understand it and I never have. I also hate the sycophants who hang around it.'*

In 1990 Diana took Prince William – then 10 – on his first walkabout in Cardiff. Afterwards she told aides: *'You know, it's strange. Every other mother in the country is warning her children not to talk to strangers and here's me telling mine that's exactly what they have to do!'*

'I don't drink at all but I understand the pressures. I'm constantly being offered drinks at parties and social functions and I know how difficult it is to resist.'

'Whenever I switch on a television soap it seems to centre around pub life. In EastEnders and Coronation Street the whole theme is drink and pubs.

'When I go out for a social evening I don't drink – but people find that peculiar.'

'In another incarnation, the last thing I would ever want to be is a horse.'

After switching on a hospital brain scanner, which promptly broke down, Diana said: *'Machines always seem to go wrong when I'm around.'*

During another hospital visit: *'I don't like needles or drips.'*

In 1990 Diana visited British military wives in Hohne, Germany and told them: *'The life of a serviceman's wife is never an easy one. I do feel for you with all my heart.'*

'William and Harry need to burn off energy playing sport – otherwise they come home and wreck the house!'

In a Cirencester music store: *'Got any Val Doonican records?'*

Speaking of the elderly, she told to her then private secretary Patrick Jephson: *'They've lived through so much, so they're really interesting.'*

'You get a lot back from them.'

'Beauty's more than skin deep you know!'

Said to her aides and personal protection officers: *'Stand by for a mood swing, boys!'*

On self-harming: *'They were desperate cries for help. I just needed time to adjust to my new position.'*

Diana talking to friend James Gilbey from the notorious Squidgy tapes recorded on New Year's Eve 1989: *'I just felt sad and empty and I thought, "Bloody hell, after all I've done for this fucking family".'*

Talking about the Queen Mother (from the Squidgy tapes): *'His grandmother is always looking at me with a strange look in her eyes. It's not hatred, it's sort of interest and pity mixed in one.'*

From the Squidgy tapes: *'If you want to be like me you have got to suffer.'*

Talking about her relationship with Charles on the tapes: *'He makes my life real, real torture, I've decided. But the distancing will be because I go out and – I hate the word – conquer the world.'*

'I don't mean that. I mean I'll go out and do my bit in the way I know how and I leave him behind.'

'That's what I see happening.'

From the Squidgy tapes: *'I know this sounds crazy, but I've lived before. Also I'm aware that people I have loved and have died and are in the spirit world looking after me.'*

'Carry out a random act of kindness with no expectation of reward, safe in the knowledge that one day someone might do the same for you.'

Letter to James Hewitt in August 1989 at height of their affair: *'I have lain awake at night loving you desperately and thanking God for bringing you into my life – you, my darling one, are the most magical and special person I've ever met and how extraordinarily lucky I am to be loved by you – what a difference it's made to me and I just long for the days when finally we will be together for always, as that is how it should be.'*

'Everyone needs to be valued. Everyone has the potential to give something back.'

'HIV doesn't make people dangerous to know, so you can shake their hands and give them a hug. Heaven knows they need it.'

'The worst illness of our time is that so many people have to suffer from never being loved.'

'What's so special about me?'

'No, it's a bore.' **On refusing to sign an autograph.**

'Family is the most important thing in the world.'

Said to her sons: *'It's not cissy to show your feelings.'*

'You can't comfort the afflicted without afflicting the comfortable.'

On William and Harry hunting shooting and fishing:
'I call them my killer Wales!'

'All William wants to do is have a gun in his hand.'

'I have a woman's instinct and it's always a good one.'

'I love going brown and never worry about getting wrinkles from too much sun.'

On her eating disorder: 'It started because Sarah [her sister] was anorexic and I idolised her so much that I wanted to be like her.'

'They say it is better to be poor and happy than rich and miserable, but how about a compromise like moderately rich and just moody?'

To a convention of child psychiatrists in 1991: 'Parents sometimes desert families, leaving their children bewildered and bereft with no explanation.'

'Many children even travel through life feeling responsible in some ways for their parents' separation.'

'To travel through life with unbalanced emotions can feel like carrying a heavy rucksack of rubbish.'

'Children are not chores but souls to love and cherish.'

'There are potential huggers in every household.'

After her infamous visit alone to the Taj Mahal as her marriage was crumbling in 1992, Diana said: 'It was a fascinating experience – very healing.'

When a reporter asked what she meant she replied:
'Work it out for yourself.'

Said to Ken Wharfe in Cairo, May 1992: *'Ken, if anything happens to me you'll let people know what I was really like, won't you?'*

In a 1992 letter to former Palace servant Cyril Dickman, Diana wrote: *'The boys are well and enjoying boarding school a lot, although Harry is constantly in trouble!'*

Just before Andrew Morton's book *Diana Her True Story,* **which blew the lid off her marriage to Charles, was published in 1992, she was sitting next to film producer David Puttnam at a dinner in Claridge's and told him:** *'Neither of us has been perfect, but I've done a really stupid thing.'*

'I have allowed a book to be written. I felt it was a good idea, a way of clearing the air, but now I think it was a very stupid thing that will cause all kinds of terrible trouble.'

'I would like to reel that movie back. It is the daftest thing I have ever done.'

'It's time to spread my wings – I'm going to fly and they cannot stop me.'

SEPARATION AND BEYOND: 1992-1997

SEPARATION AND BEYOND: 1992-1997

Note posted on her desk at Kensington Palace: *'Greatest barrier to bonding is low self-esteem itself.'*

'A woman with low self-esteem may choose to live without intimacy.'

'She might be terrified of letting someone get too close lest they discover the "real" her and reject.'

'I will always bring love wherever I go in the world, to whomever: leper, AIDS patient, king, queen or president. That's why the suits don't like me – because I get on better with the people "downstairs" than I do "upstairs".'

'We're all equal, regardless of where we've got to in life. Daddy taught me that.'

During 1992 and 1993 Diana poured her heart out in a series of taped interviews with her voice coach, Peter Settelen, which were broadcast after her death.

'My father-in-law said to my husband, "Uh, if your marriage doesn't work out, you can always go back to her [Camilla Parker Bowles] *after five years," which is exactly what happened.'*

'The odd thing was, when I was bulimic, I wasn't angry, because the anger, I thought, was coming out that way. And it always felt better after I'd been sick… I'd be very passive afterwards, very quiet.' Told to Settelen.

'I can't bear people to say, "we understand" – nobody understands unless you're the individual concerned.'

In the Settelen tapes Diana made the extraordinary confession that in the mid-1980s she fell in love with her police bodyguard Barry Mannakee.

'He was the greatest fellow I have ever had.'

'I was only happy when he was around.'

'I was quite happy to give it all up… just to go off and live with him.

'*Can you believe it? And he kept saying he thought it was a good idea too.*'

'*He'd tell me I looked good, something my husband no longer did.*'

Mannakee was moved from protecting Diana and in 1987 was killed in a motorbike accident. '*I think he was bumped off but I will never know,*' **she told Settelen.**

'*I should never have played with fire but I did, and I got burned.*'

Asked by Settelen why she did so much charity work she replied, laughing: '*I've got nothing else to do!*' **She then added:** '*It's a very good question, I don't know an answer.*'

'*My parents never said they loved me.*'

'*I knew that something profound was coming my way and I was treading water, waiting for it.*'

'*I didn't know what it was. I didn't know if it was coming next year or next month.*'

'*But I knew I was different from my friends in where I was going.*'

On her stepmother Raine: *'I wanted to throttle that stepmother of mine because she brought such grief. She kept saying to me, "Oh but Diana, you're so unhappy in your own marriage, you're just jealous of Daddy's and my relationship".'*

'Jealousy was not high on the agenda – it was behaviour I was after.'

'I know that one day – if I play the rules of life, the game of life – I will be able to have those things which I've always pined for and they will be that much more special because I will be that much older and be able to appreciate them much more.'

'I think from day one I always knew I would never be the next Queen, put it that way.'

'I had so many dreams as a young girl… hopes that my husband would look after me, he'd be like a father figure, he'd support me, encourage me, say, "Well done," but I didn't get any of that.'

'They wanted a fairy princess to come and touch them and everything would turn into gold.'

'Little did they realise that the individual was crucifying herself inside because she didn't think she was good enough.'

Told to voice coach Peter Settelen in 1992: *'I was always told by my family that I was the thick one. That I was stupid and my brother was the clever one. And I was always so conscious of that. I used to go to the headmistress crying, saying I wish I wasn't so stupid.'*

'I didn't like myself. I was ashamed because I couldn't cope with the pressures... I felt compelled to perform.'

'The day I walked down the aisle at St Paul's Cathedral, I felt that my personality was taken away from me, and I was taken over by the royal machine.'

'From now on, I am going to own myself and be true to myself. I no longer want to live someone else's idea of what and who I should be.'

'I am going to be me.'

Said to her hairstylist Natalie Symons: (on Andrew and Fergie) *'Why did they bother to get divorced? They shouldn't have done it because they'll never really split up.'*

'I made so many balls-ups trying to be like Fergie. I went to a pop concert in leather trousers which I thought was frightfully "with it", completely putting out of my mind that I was the future Queen.'

'I have it on very good authority that the quest for perfection in society can leave the individual gasping for breath at every turn.'

Said to women at a family refuge in Chiswick, London, March 1993: 'From early childhood many had felt they were expected to be perfect, but didn't feel they had the right to express their true feelings to those around them – feelings of guilt, of self-revulsion and low personal esteem. Well ladies, we all know what men can be like, don't we?'

Speech about women and children with AIDS in September 1993: 'These children need to feel the same things as other children. To play, to laugh and cry, to make friends, to enjoy the ordinary experiences of childhood. To feel loved and nurtured and included by the world they live in, without the stigma that AIDS continues to attract.'

'Anywhere I see suffering, that is where I want to be, doing what I can.'

'If I'm going to talk on behalf of any cause, I want to go and see the problem for myself and learn about it.'

'I don't want expensive gifts; I don't want to be bought. I have everything I want. I just want someone to be there for me, to make me feel safe and secure.'

Speech on women and mental health in June 1993:
'Each person is born with very individual qualities and potential. We as a society owe it to women to create a truly supportive environment in which they too can grow and move forward.'

When she looked out of her window at Kensington Palace and saw her neighbour, Austrian-born Princess Michael of Kent, she said: *'The Waffen SS are on the march!'*

On being followed by the paparazzi: *'It's like living in a goldfish bowl with all these people coming to look at you and you're just there swimming around in circles with no escape.'*

Speech to the Headway charity in December 1993:
'When I started my public life, twelve years ago, I understood the media might be interested in what I did. I realised then their attention would inevitably focus on both our private and public lives.'

'But I was not aware of how overwhelming that attention would become. Nor to the extent to which it would affect both my public duties and my personal life, in a manner that's been hard to bear.'

'At the end of this year, when I've completed my diary of official engagements, I will be reducing the extent of the public life I've lead so far.'

'I hope you can find it in your hearts to understand and to give me the time and space that has been lacking in recent years.'

Said to a group of women in 1993: *'The kindness and affection from the public have carried me through some of the most difficult periods and always your love and affection have eased the journey.'*

Said to friends in 1994: *'I live for my sons… I would be lost without them.'*

Diana helped bury her friend Rosa Monckton's stillborn baby in the garden of Kensington Palace in the spring of 1994. She told her butler Paul Burrell: *'If we're asked, we'll say my friends are burying a pet.'*

'The only problem is people will find this baby one day and say it was mine.'

On rumours that James Hewitt was Prince Harry's father, Diana told healer Simone Simmons: *'If people worked the dates out properly they would see that it's nothing to do with Hewitt. It's pretty obvious that he's a Windsor. In colouring he is a Spencer but he has Charles's eyes.'*

Told to then *Times* Editor Peter Stothard at lunch: *'John Major and my husband are both very alike, quite BFs* [best friends] *these days, always seeing each other.'*

To Peter Stothard: *'My husband's father once sent me a long formal letter setting out the duties of the Princess of Wales. There was "much more to it than being popular," he said.'*

'I sent him back a long letter in reply. He sent a shorter one – and so on until I finally signed off with, "It's been so nice getting to know you like this".'

On Prince William: *'Isn't he gorgeous – he's so tall. I call him DDG – drop-dead gorgeous.'*

'It's vital the monarchy keeps in touch with the people – it's what I try to do.'

On the Queen: *'I admire her. I long to get inside her mind and talk to her.'*

To a close friend on why she watched heart operations: *'If I am to care for people in hospital I really must know every aspect of their treatment and to understand their suffering.'*

'I love to hold people's hands when I visit hospitals, even though they are sometimes shocked because they haven't

experienced anything like it before, but to me it's a normal thing to do.'

'Don't call me an icon. I'm just a mother trying to help.'

'If I was ever washed up on a desert island, the one luxury I would crave would be my mascara.'

Said to Madonna at their only, brief, meeting in 1995: *'I think you handle the press better than I do.'*

Told over lunch to Tina Brown: *'I'm very good at sorting people's heads out.'*

'I don't mind people using my name as long as it's for a good cause.'

On catering for herself when the staff were off: *'Marks and Spencer have got these very clever little meals that you just put in the microwave and you put the timer on and press the button, and it's done for you!'*

After falling in love with Pakistani heart surgeon Dr Hasnat Khan, she told her hair-stylist Natalie Symonds: *'He's such a brilliant surgeon and so dedicated. He has saved so many people's lives, I admire him so much.'*

'Isn't he drop-dead gorgeous?'

'He works so hard and can't see me as often as I'd like, so I just live for his late night phone calls. But after I've talked to him I can't sleep because I'm so happy and excited.'

After watching Dr Khan perform heart surgery:
'Sometimes I want to throw up but I keep watching. You wouldn't believe it, I saw this man's chest cut open from the top to the bottom.'

On watching the operations: 'It motivates me – it brings purpose and meaning to my life.'

On Khan, she told Natalie Symonds: 'He hasn't any money, I'll have to keep him. But I've got a thing about doctors!'

'He's insecure and I'm insecure, so we have a lot in common.'

'I'm no longer lonely, I know what love is now.'

Just before her sensational *Panorama* interview was broadcast in November 1995 she told her private secretary Patrick Jepson: 'It's really good Patrick – don't worry, everything's going to be all right.'

'Grown men have seen it and it moved them to tears.'

From the *Panorama* interview with Martin Bashir. Responding to the question: *'Do you think Mrs Parker Bowles was a factor in the breakdown of your marriage?'* **Diana answered:** *'Well, there were three of us in the marriage, so it was a bit crowded.'*

'She won't go quietly, that's the problem. I'll fight to the end, because I believe that I have a role to fulfil, and I've got two children to bring up.'

Admitting she had an affair with Captain James Hewitt: *'Yes, I adored him, yes I was in love with him. But I was very let down.'*

Also from the *Panorama* interview: *'I always knew I'd never be the next queen. I'd like to be a queen of people's hearts, in people's hearts, but I don't see myself being queen of this country.'*

'I don't think many people will want me to be queen.'

'I think that I've always been the eighteen-year-old girl he [**Charles**] *got engaged to, so I don't think I've been given any credit for growth. And, my goodness, I've had to grow.'*

'Nobody ever said a thing, never said, "Well done" or "Was it OK?" But if I tripped up, which inevitably I did, because I was new at the game, a ton of bricks came down on me.'

'There's no better way to dismantle a personality than to isolate it.'

'It's a very demanding role being Prince of Wales, but it's an equally more demanding role being king.'

'And because I know the character, I would think that the top job, as I call it, would bring enormous limitations to him, and I don't know whether he could adapt to that.'

'My wish is that my husband finds peace of mind.'

Panorama: 'I do things differently, because I don't go by a rule book, because I lead from the heart, not the head, and albeit that's got me into trouble in my work, I understand that.'

'I want my boys to have an understanding of people's emotions, their insecurities, people's distress, and their hopes and dreams.'

'When I used to sit on hospital beds and hold people's hands, people were shocked. They said they'd never seen this before, but to me it was a normal thing to do. And when I saw the reassurance that an action like that gave, I did it everywhere, and will always do that.'

'Friends on my husband's side were indicating that I was
again unstable, sick, and should be put in a home of some
sort in order to get better. I was almost an embarrassment.'

'I think I was so fed up with being seen as someone who
was a basket case because I am a very strong person and I
know that causes complications in the system that I live in.'

On why she gave her Panorama interview: 'What must
it be like for a little boy to read that daddy never loved
mummy?'

'I want to reassure all those people who have loved me and
supported me throughout the last fifteen years that I've
never let them down.'

'The man on the street, yup, because that's what matters to
me more than anything else.'

'I like to be a free spirit. Some don't like that, but that's the
way I am.'

Asked if she gambled, she replied: 'Not with cards... but
with life.'

'I get a lot of infections because I spend so much time with
sick people.'

On sending Prince William to Eton: *'There's no messing around at Eton about someone being heir to the throne. If you're not popular, charming, intelligent, or good at games, you're not going to rate are you?'*

According to healer Simone Simmons, Diana had a fling with John Kennedy Jr in 1995 and told her: *'He was an amazing lover – a ten, the tops.'*

After a tour of the White House: *'I would have loved it there.'*

An infamous letter she wrote to herself in October 1995: *'I am sitting here at my desk today in October, longing for someone to hug me and encourage me to keep strong and hold my head high.'*

'This particular phase in my life is the most dangerous.'

'My husband is planning "an accident" in my car, brake failure and serious injury in order to make the path clear for Charles to marry.'

'I have been battered, bruised, and abused mentally by a system for fifteen years now, but I feel no resentment, I carry no hatred.'

'I am weary of the battles, but I will never surrender.'

'I am strong inside and maybe that is a problem for my enemies.'

'Thank you, Charles, for putting me through such hell and for giving me the opportunity to learn from the cruel things you have done to me.'

'I have gone forward fast and have cried more than anyone will ever know.'

'The anguish nearly killed me, but my inner strength has never let me down, and my guides have taken such good care of me up there.'

'Aren't I fortunate to have their wings to protect me.'

On a visit to Japan in 1995 she told her private secretary Patrick Jephson: 'It's very important to wear really high heels. I'm already taller than the Emperor, but it won't do any harm to look just that bit taller!'

After her mother gave an interview without consulting her, Diana told healer Simone Simmons: 'I hate her.'

She also said of Frances Shand Kydd: 'She made me feel as if I should never have been born.'
The pair were not on speaking terms when Diana died.

At the 1995 staff Christmas party at the Lanesborough Hotel in London, Diana approached William and Harry's nanny, Tiggy Legge-Bourke, whom she suspected of having an affair with her estranged husband, Prince Charles, and told her: *'Sorry to hear you lost the baby.'*
There was no foundation to her comment.

To gossip columnist Taki Theodoracopulos at a 1995 party: *'Do you think I'm mad?'*

'I found in the end that therapy was pointless for me, because the people trying to help me hadn't been through what I had been through. In some cases, I ended up thinking it was they who needed help, not me.'

On US President Bill Clinton: *'He's got a Southern drawl that sounds incredibly sexy, but I'm not so keen on Hillary – she's quite cold.'*

'I want a flat stomach and a proper waistline.'

On the Royal Family: *'They don't have friendships – they have allies. They are a tribe and their instinct is tribal.'*

As divorce loomed Diana was in a meeting with Prince Philip who told her: *'If you don't behave, my girl, we'll take your title away.'*

Diana replied: *'My title is a lot older than yours,'* referring to the lineage of the Spencer family.

'It's the 28th August 1996 – fifteen years of marriage have now been signed off,' Diana wrote on the day after her divorce was finalised.

Shortly after her divorce, she told her butler Paul Burrell: *'Make a list of everything we need. Let's spend a bit more of HIS money while we can!'*

'I never wanted a divorce and always dreamed of a happy marriage with loving support from Charles.'

'Although that was never meant to be, we do have two wonderful boys who are deeply loved by their parents.'

'A part of me will always love Charles, but how I wish he'd looked after me and been proud of my work.'

'It has been a turbulent fifteen years, having to face the envy, jealousy and hatred from Charles's friends and family – they have so misunderstood me and that has been painful and brought enormous heartache.'

'My husband made me feel so inadequate in every possible way that each time I came up for air he pushed me down again.'

On Charles and Camilla Parker Bowles: *'Oh, I don't care. They can get married, they probably ought to get married, it doesn't bother me now.'* **Told to royal biographer Anthony Holden over lunch.**

"How on earth could I lose out to a girl who has bad teeth from smoking and dandruff?"

'My father always told me never to talk to strangers. And I've spent the last fifteen years doing nothing but talk to strangers!'

To fundraiser Marie Sutton in Sydney, Australia: *'Someone is always following me. The paparazzi are on my tail everywhere I go. It is getting to the point where no human being should have to endure what happens to me.'*

Asked by Marie why she didn't 'get out', Diana replied: *'There is no way out. I am William's mother and I have to look after him.'*

'I have to go on, no matter how awful my life has become.'

'I have to stick with it for the sake of my boys. Perhaps their lives will be better than mine. That's the only thing that keeps me going.'

She also told Marie: *'I only ever asked for help once from the Queen. I asked her to speak to my husband and persuade him to end his affair with Camilla – not just for my sake, but for the family, for all our sakes. But she refused to help me.'*

'She said she couldn't intervene. After that, I never asked for anything ever again.'

'Life is mostly froth and bubble, two things stand in stone: kindness in another's trouble, courage in your own.'

Diana told writer Shirley Conran that she could not offer William and Harry anything that could compete with holidays at Balmoral. *'They do all those manly, killing things – and there's that wonderful go-kart track.'*

Told to Tina Brown: *'All my hopes are on William now. I'm hoping he will grow up to be as smart handling the media as John Kennedy Jr.'*

'The births of both of my sons were specially induced to fit in with my husband's polo games.'

'I was sick all the time when pregnant with Harry. At one point I was throwing up so often, I didn't know if it was morning sickness or bulimia.'

In January 1997 Diana flew to Angola to draw attention to the horrors of land mines. *'The international community must work together for an end to the use of these weapons,'* **she said in a speech.**

'Because I have this power, I have to use it.'

'It's appalling the damage they do, and no one cares and they just spray them all over the place like ghastly bulbs. At least I can do something good with this kind of presence, you know, the opportunities I have, well, they're not opportunities, they're huge open gateways...'

'Those children! Those poor limbless children! I can't get them out of my mind. When I go to bed at night they are all I can think about.'

When some politicians criticised her for getting 'involved in politics' she said: *'I was only trying to highlight a problem going on all around the world.'*

'I am not a political figure, I am a humanitarian figure, always was, always will be.'

On return from Angola she told close friends about Hasnat Khan: *'I am going to marry him.'*

Talking to Meredith Etherington-Smith, marketing director of Christie's Worldwide, who was organising new photos of Diana, taken by Mario Testino: *'I want to look how I feel inside.'*

'I feel I belong to the 20th century now, I really do. I'm doing modern things and I'm trying to lead a modern life, and I'm a single woman and that's how I want to look.'

After the photo shoot with Testino in a Battersea, London studio Diana said: *'It was one of the happiest days of my life – and I really mean it.'*

On the photos she said: *'These are me, really, really me.'* *'God, I think I look like Marilyn Monroe in those pictures.'*

'Who would take me on?'

On1 July 1997, her 36th and last birthday, Diana was to attend a dinner at the Tate Gallery. Her hairstylist Natalie Symons asked her if she planned to drink champagne to celebrate.
'I never drink alcohol,' said Diana. *'There's been too much of it in my family.*

'*I am spending the evening of my birthday in a room full of people I don't know and don't even like. The only person there that I know will be my brother. What a way to enjoy my birthday!*'

After her 1996 divorce, Diana's behaviour became increasingly erratic, and she decided to dispense with her Scotland Yard protection officers.

When fashion designer Gianni Versace was murdered in 1997, she was on holiday with the Al Fayeds aboard their yacht *Jonikal*. '*Do you think they'll do that to me?*' she asked Dodi Fayed's bodyguard, Lee Sansum.

On a trip to Rome with her Argentinian friend Roberto Devorik, she spotted a portrait of Prince Philip on a wall and told him: '*He hates me. He really hates me and would like to see me disappear.*'

She went on: '*I am a threat in their eyes. They only use me when they need me for official functions and then they drop me again in the darkness.*'

'*They are not going to kill me by poisoning me or in a big plane where others will get hurt.*'

'*They will do it when I am in a small plane, in a car when I'm driving, or in a helicopter.*'

Also to Devorik: *'Roberto, you are so naive. Don't you see, they took my HRH title and now they are slowly taking my kids. They are now letting me know when I can have the children.'*

Said to former lover James Hewitt in summer of 1997, shortly before she died: *'I'm going to shock the world and run off and marry a big fat black man.'*

On a visit to Angola in 1997: *'The greatest problem in the world today is intolerance. Everyone is so intolerant of each other.'*

A few weeks before her death Diana told journalist and author Ingrid Seward: *'He [Charles] loved me when we got married and I loved him. We still love each other now, in a different way. At least, I love him.'*

'It is very sad about our marriage.'

Said to journalists following her on holiday with the Al Fayeds in the South of France, July 1997: *'You will have a big surprise coming soon, you'll see, with the next thing I do.'*

After Diana began her summer romance with Dodi Fayed, she told hairstylist Tess Rock: *'I love his exotic accent. I love the way he says "Di-yana, you're so naughty!"'*

Said to friend Lady Elsa Bowker shortly before her death: *'When you are happy you can forgive a great deal.'*

To Cindy Crawford shortly before the tragedy in Paris: *'Dodi is a fantastic man. He covers me with attention and with care.'*

'I feel newly loved.'

'Whatever I do, it's never going to be enough for some people.'

When asked what she would like as an epitaph on her grave: *'A great hope crushed in its infancy.'*

'If you find someone you love in your life, then hang on to that love.'

'Just being kind is all the sad world needs.'

'There has to be more to our existence than actually meets the eye.'

Diana, Princess of Wales
1961–1997

TIMELINE OF DIANA'S LIFE

- Born 1 July 1961 at Park House, Sandringham, Norfolk.

- Her father, the eighth Earl Spencer and his wife Frances, separated in 1967 and divorced in 1969.

- After a whirlwind romance beginning in 1980, she and Prince Charles announced their engagement on 24 February 1981.

- They were married on 29 July 1981 in St Paul's Cathedral, with 600,000 people lining the streets and a billion watching on TV around the world.

- Diana gave birth to their first son, Prince William, on 21 June 1982.

- Prince Harry was born on 15 September 1984.

- On 9 December 1992, British Prime Minister John Major announced that Charles and Diana were separating.

- They were divorced on 28 August 1996.

- On 31 August 1997 Diana died from injuries sustained in a car crash in Paris, along with her then boyfriend Dodi Fayed, and the driver of the Mercedes, Henri Paul.